Paul thurlby

NUMBERS

Hodder Children's Books

A division of Hachette Children's Books

O
ZERO

I started working on Numbers the year after I had finished Alphabet. It immediately became apparent that attaching meaning to numbers would prove more of a challenge than the alphabet. Not to mention the fact that maths was one of my least favourite subjects at school. I hope I have succeeded, where my teacher Mr Housden failed, in making numbers fun. In the end, I really enjoyed working on this book.

Originally from Nottingham, now based in London, I have been working as a full-time illustrator since 2006. I hold my pen in an unusual manner and was never 'corrected' by any teachers at school.

I work on commissions in advertising, publishing, editorial and design for clients including The Southbank Centre, The Guardian, The French Tourist Board, It's Nice That, Nineteen Seventy Three Ltd, Templar Publishing, Vanity Fair, The New Yorker and Warner/Chappell.

My inspiration comes from mid-century design and illustration. My work has been described as being retro-modern. I use old books, postcards and pieces of paper for the backgrounds. Often, for example, I will buy an old book from a charity shop just to use its back page.

For my sister, Tina; and nieces Natalie, Eryn and Francesca.

WWW.PAULTHURLBY.COM

FIRST PUBLISHED IN 2014 BY HODDER CHILDREN'S BOOKS
COPYRIGHT © PAUL THURLBY 2014
HODDER CHILDREN'S BOOKS, 338 EUSTON ROAD, LONDON NW1 3BH
HODDER CHILDREN'S BOOKS AUSTRALIA, LEVEL 17/207 KENT STREET, SYDNEY NSW 2000
THE RIGHT OF PAUL THURLBY TO BE IDENTIFIED AS THE AUTHOR AND ILLUSTRATOR OF THIS WORK HAS BEEN ASSERTED BY
HIM IN ACCORDANCE WITH THE COPYRIGHT, DESIGNS AND PATENTS ACT 1988. ALL RIGHTS RESERVED.
A CATALOGUE RECORD OF THIS BOOK IS AVAILABLE FROM THE BRITISH LIBRARY.
ISBN: 978 1 444 91875 5
PRINTED IN CHINA
HODDER CHILDREN'S BOOKS IS A DIVISION OF HACHETTE CHILDREN'S BOOKS. AN HACHETTE UK COMPANY. WWW.HACHETTE.CO.UK

1
ONE

number one

2
TWO

3
THREE

THREE d

4
FOUR

The FabFOUR

5
FIVE

HIGH FIVE

6
SIX

7
SEVEN

Snappy SEVEN

8
EIGHT

9

NINE

Nine *lives*

10
TEN

Perfect **TEN**

20
TWENTY

TWENTY

MILES PER HOUR

30
THIRTY

40
FORTY

FORTY L♥VE

50
FIFTY

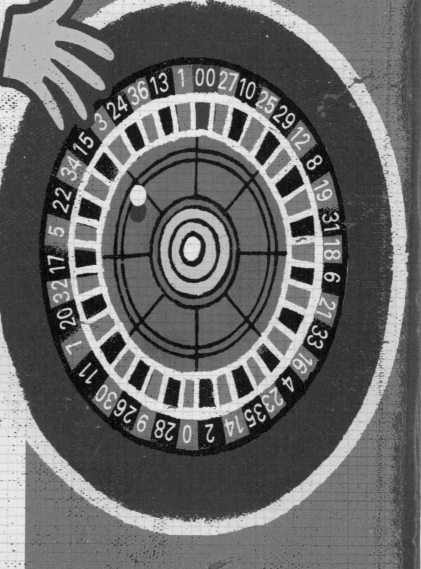

60
SIXTY

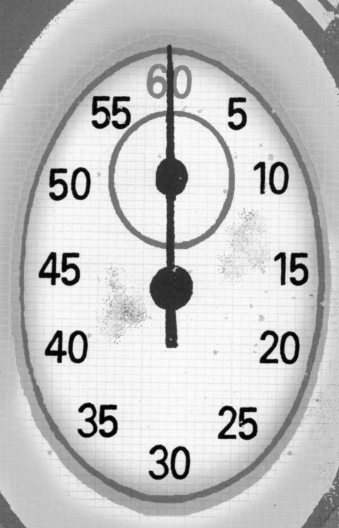

SIXTY SECONDS

70
SEVENTY

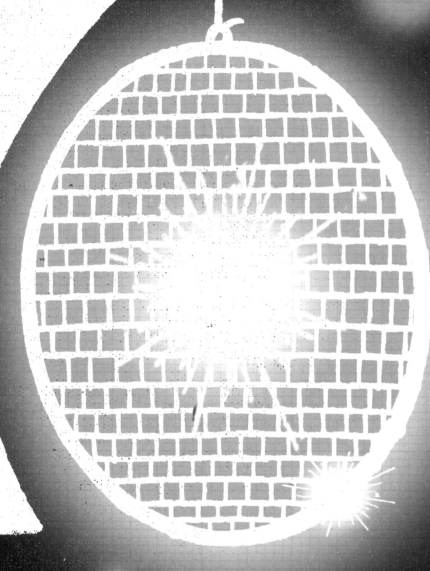

70

DISCO SEVENTY

80
EIGHTY

HOTEL AURORE
PARIS

GRAND HOTEL
PRAHA

AROUND THE WORLD IN

EIGHTY
DAYS

90
NINETY

NINETY DEGREES

100

ONE
HUNDRED

ONE HUNDRED
PER CENT